Dime-Store Alchemy

Joseph Cornell by Hans Namuth

Dime–Store Alchemy

THE ART OF

JOSEPH CORNELL

CHARLES SIMIC

NEW YORK REVIEW BOOKS

New York

This is a New York Review Book
Published by The New York Review of Books
1755 Broadway, New York, NY 10019
www.nyrb.com

Cover illustration: Joesph Cornell, *Medici Slot Machine*, 1942, private collection; courtesy The Menil Collection, Houston. © The Joseph and Robert Cornell Memorial Foundation; licensed by VAGA, New York, NY. Photograph by Hickey-Robertson, Houston.

Library of Congress Cataloging-in-Publication Data
Simic, Charles, 1938–
  Dime-store alchemy : the art of Joseph Cornell / by Charles Simic.
    p. cm. — (New York Review Books classics)
  Originally published: Hopewell, N.J. : Ecco Press, 1992.
  Includes bibliographical references.
  ISBN 1-59017-170-5 (alk. paper)
  1. Cornell, Joseph—Criticism and interpretation. 2. Surrealism—United States. I. Cornell, Joseph. II. Title.
  N6537.C66S57 2006
  709.2—dc22
                                        2006020672
ISBN-13: 978-1-59017-170-7
ISBN-10: 1-59017-170-5

Printed in the United States of America on acid-free paper.
10 9 8 7 6 5 4 3 2 1

Contents

Illustrations

5. Untitled (Bébé Marie), early 1940s.
   Construction, 23½ x 12³/₈ x 5¼ in. Collection, The Museum of Modern Art, New York. Acquired through the Lillie P. Bliss Bequest.

6. Untitled (*Pink Palace*), ca. 1946–1948.
   Box construction, 10 x 16³/₈ x 3¾ in. The Robert Lehman Art Trust.

7. Untitled (Soap Bubble Set), 1936.
   Glass case with inserts, 15¾ x 14¼ x 5³/₈ in. Wadsworth Atheneum, Hartford, Connecticut. Gift of Henry and Walter Keney.

8. *The Hotel Eden*, 1945.
   Construction, 15¹/₈ x 15¾ x 4¾ in. National Gallery of Canada, Ottawa.

Preface

I HAVE a dream in which Joseph Cornell and I pass each other on the street. This is not beyond the realm of possibility. I walked the same New York neighborhoods that he did between 1958 and 1970. I was either working at lowly office jobs, or I was out of work spending my days in the Public Library on Forty-second Street which Cornell frequented himself. I don't remember when it was that I first saw his shadow boxes. When I was young, I was interested in surrealism, so it's likely that I came across his name and the reproduction of his art that way. Cornell made me feel that I should do something like that myself as a poet, but for a long time I continued to admire him without knowing much about him. Only after his death did he become an obsession with me. Of course, much had already been written about him, and most of it was excellent. Cornell's originality and modesty disarm the critics and make them sympathetic and unusually perceptive. When it comes to his art, our eyes and imagination are the best guides. In writing the pieces for this book, I hoped to emulate his way of working and come to understand him that way. It is worth pointing out that Cornell worked in the absence of any aesthetic theory and previous notion of beauty. He shuffled a few inconsequential found objects inside his boxes until together they composed an image that pleased him with no clue as to what that image will turn out to be in the end. I had hoped to do the same.

Chronology

JOSEPH CORNELL was born on December 24, 1903, in Nyack, a town on the Hudson River. His parents, Joseph Cornell and Helen Ten Broeck Storms, were descendants of old Dutch families. They had three other children after Joseph; daughters Elizabeth and Helen, and finally a second son, Robert, born in 1910, who suffered from cerebral palsy.

The Cornells were a moderately well-to-do family. The father worked many years for a wholesale woolen manufacturer, a job in which he went from being a salesman to designing textiles. Both the father and the mother were interested in the arts. They were musically inclined and loved theater. Cornell's mother was an avid reader who even wrote a movie scenario. In 1917, however, the father died of leukemia and the family's financial circumstances became strained. Mrs. Cornell took part-time jobs making sweaters and cakes. Still, she managed to send Joseph to Phillips Academy, in Andover, Massachusetts, where he spent the years 1917–1919.

At Phillips, Cornell studied sciences and Romance

languages but did not distinguish himself as a student. He did not complete the prescribed course of study and therefore failed to receive a diploma. Back in New York his family was now living in Bayside, Queens, and Cornell went to work to support them. Thanks to family connections he got a job with a textile manufacturer with offices on Madison Square. From 1921 to 1931, he peddled woolen samples door to door in the manufacturing district in lower Manhattan.

Walking around the city and killing time between appointments, Cornell foraged in used bookstores and junk shops. He started collecting books, records, photographs, prints, theatrical memorabilia, and collected prints of old movies. He went to art galleries during the day and to the opera and ballet at night. This appears to be a period of considerable soul-searching for Cornell, culminating in his conversion to Christian Science.

In 1929 the family purchased the small frame house in Bayside. In the basement of that house, where Cornell lived till his death, he made all his art.

In 1931 Cornell discovered the Julian Levy gallery. One day he watched the owner unpack the surrealist objects and paintings that had been sent over from France for an exhibition at Hartford's Wadsworth Atheneum. A few weeks later, Cornell came back to the gallery and showed Levy two-dimensional collages, what he called "montages." Levy liked them immediately, encouraged Cornell to make more, and included his work in an exhibition of surrealist art in January 1932.

The period of 1932–1936 was one of experimentation

for Cornell. He tried various kinds of boxes—prefabricated ones, round ones, paperboard ones—and finally began to make his own. In the same period he wrote a filmscript, *Monsieur Phot*, and made his first movie, *Rose Hobart*, a cinema collage made up of spliced old film. He met Marcel Duchamp and exhibited in the Museum of Modern Art's exhibition entitled Fantastic Art, Dada, Surrealism.

In the late 1930s Cornell was employed as a textile designer. He also did freelance design for *Vogue* and *House and Garden* and wrote for *View* and *Dance Index*. The editors of these magazines knew of his vast collection of photographs, prints, and theatrical memorabilia.

During the Second World War many French artists and writers were exiled in New York, and Cornell met many of them. Max Ernst and Matta even visited his basement studio. Cornell's work became more serial—that is, he now worked on boxes that repeated and varied certain images.

After the war his art was shown in a number of important exhibitions. He made other films and by the late 1950s started to hire assistants to help him with his work. Although by this time he knew just about everybody in the art world, he kept his distance. Though European themes and foreign language phrases often appeared in his work, it is worth noting that Cornell, after leaving Andover, never traveled beyond the New York city area.

In the final decade of his life (1962–1972) his production declined as his reputation here and abroad grew.

His brother, Robert, died in 1965, and his mother in 1966. Cornell continued to live alone in his house. He described himself in that period as "semi-retired," although he went on working with assistants and corresponding with a large number of people. He died at his home on December 20, 1972, of heart failure. Earlier that day, he told his sister on the phone, "I wish I had not been so reserved."

Acknowledgments

Parts of this book were first published in *The Yale Review* and *Epoch*, to whose editors grateful acknowledgment is made.

Permission to reproduce the works of Joseph Cornell has been granted by The Joseph and Robert Cornell Memorial Foundation and licensed by VAGA, New York, NY.

Excerpts from the papers of Joseph Cornell were made courtesy of the Archives of American Art–Smithsonian Institution. The entries included were taken from microfilm reels 1058–1077.

I

Medici Slot Machine

Me? I pursue an image, no more.

—Gérard de Nerval

A white pigeon pecking on the marble steps of the library watched over by two stone lions. It's like a dream, I thought.

Next, I saw it on the table of the storefront fortune-teller pecking the eyes of the king of hearts.

Next, it perched on the shoulder of a black man riding a bicycle at daybreak down Sixth Avenue.

MISS DELPHINE

On the streets Cornell walked forty years ago, there were still medical leech dealers; importers of armadillo meat and ostrich eggs. There were people like Miss Delphine Binger, who collected goose, turkey, and chicken wishbones so she could boil them and polish them and then decorate them with charms and ribbons. She sent them to presidents, movie stars, famous politicians in the same way Cornell sent gifts of scraps of paper and odd objects to ballerinas he loved.

THE MAN ON THE DUMP

He looked the way I imagine Melville's Bartleby to have looked the day he gave up his work to stare at the blank wall outside the office window.

There are always such men in cities. Solitary wanderers in long-outmoded overcoats, they sit in modest restaurants and side-street cafeterias eating a soft piece of cake. They are deadly pale, have tired eyes, and their lapels are covered with crumbs. Once they were something else, now they work as office messengers. With a large yellow envelope under one arm, they climb the stairs to the tenth floor when the elevator is out of order. They keep their hands in their pockets even in summertime. Any one of them could be Cornell.

He was a descendant of an old New York Dutch family that had grown impoverished after his father's early death. He lived with his mother and invalid brother in a small frame house on Utopia Parkway in Queens and roamed the streets of Manhattan in seeming idleness. A devout Christian Scientist, he was a recluse and an eccentric who admired the writings of French Romantic and Symbolist poets. His great hero was Gérard de Nerval, famous for promenading the streets of Paris with a live lobster on a leash.

WHAT CORNELL DID ON
JANUARY 24, 1947

Shaved and dressed and waved good-bye to Robert on porch (Mother shopping). Waved to Robert from train. So far uneventful but rest of day picked up that kind of richness in which a revelling in detail becomes such a feast of experience—went all the way in to Penn Station. Just before going under tunnel looked up at freight cars—the word Jane scrawled on a box-car in large letters, red with a touch of pink, then touches of primary colors mingling with a scene of men working on the tracks with a long crane mounted on a car—all over in a flash but evoking a strong feeling—had not remembered anything just like that at that point—but similar varied combinations many times from the elevated viewpoint of the subway before going under at same point (the puffing locos, omnipresent pigeons, markings on cars in freight yard, etc. Once in awhile a touch like the above. This enhanced by a touch of spring in the air. Sunny. Took bus (1:30) to 42 & 11 Ave.—feeling of great felicity in large corner caferteria with aspect of dog-wagon. Griddle cakes, coffee, apple pie a la mode. Walked up 11 Ave to clear up my film at Major Labs where for almost ten years M. Francis Doublier, the pioneer Lumière cameraman, has accomodated me.

Went up in freight elevator and got glimpses into different floors not afforded by passenger elevator (out of order) of workers in grimy industrial plants. Remembered with vividness the days of George Boyce and the early movies acquired from him. Took bus crosstown and lingered before appointment at Vogue, *4:00. Found Jenny Lind song sheet, La Sonmambula, and colored feathers in dime store. Boxes got good reception. Up to 59th. St. windfall of Bibliotècque Rose to cover etuis, Souvenirs containing good Gérard de Nerval (DeCampo), an original colored Deveria of a standing oriental woman musician— two heroic sized forest prints for owl boxes—unusual feeling of satisfaction and accomplishment, unexpected and more abiding than usual.*

THE ROMANTIC MOVEMENT

Poe has a story called "The Man of the Crowd" in which a recently discharged hospital patient sits in a coffee shop in London, enjoying his freedom, and watching the evening crowd, when he notices a decrepit old man of unusual appearance and behavior whom he decides to follow. The man at first appears to be hurrying with a purpose. He crosses and recrosses the city until the aimlessness of his walking eventually becomes obvious to his pursuer. He walks all night through the now-deserted streets, and is still walking as the day breaks. His pursuer follows him all of the next day and abandons him only as the shades of the second evening come on. Before he does, he confronts the stranger, looks him steadfastly in the eye, but the stranger does not acknowledge him and resumes his walk.

Poe's is one of the great odes to the mystery of the city. Who among us was not once that pursuer or that stranger? Cornell followed shop girls, waitresses, young students "who had a look of innocence." I myself remember a tall man of uncommon handsomeness who walked on Madison Avenue with eyes tightly closed as if he were listening to music. He bumped into people, but since he was well dressed, they didn't seem to mind.

"How wild a history," says Poe's narrator, "is written within that bosom." On a busy street one quickly becomes a voyeur. An air of danger, eroticism, and crushing solitude play hide-and-seek in the crowd. The indeterminate, the unforeseeable, the ethereal, and the fleeting rule there. The city is the place where the most unlikely opposites come together, the place where our separate intuitions momentarily link up. The myth of Theseus, the Minotaur, Ariadne, and her thread continue here. The city is a labyrinth of analogies, the Symbolist forest of correspondences.

Like a comic-book Spider-Man, the solitary voyeur rides the web of occult forces.

UNTITLED (LE PIANO), CA. 1948

Isn't there a story about a man in prison who drew a keyboard on a piece of cardboard paper, the white and black keys in proper order, and then spent hours playing the silent piano?

This, too, is a magical piano. It has a blue-faced cupid and what looks like an electric bell. It has a score —something romantic—but no keys. There are also two matchboxes covered with music notes, and that's about it.

In the villa by the sea Seraphina played the silent piano.

Little night music for the eyes.

THE METHOD OF SEERS

Cornell made notes on scraps of paper:

Into the city and all the way up to the museum of the American Indian to find it closed! Compensation in the buoyant feeling aroused by the buildings of the Geographical Society in their quiet uptown setting. An abstract feeling of geography and voyaging I have thought about before of getting into objects, like the Compass Set with map.

Lexington and 24th. Goldsmith's assortment. Mexican midget, dancing bear. Hungarian cards. Bay of Naples lithograph colored.

APRIL 16, 1946 (TUESDAY)
    Blustery but pleasant—an exceptionally fine atmosphere—(magical, theatrical).

Vaguest recall of an elegant cockatoo at dusk 14th St.

WHERE CHANCE MEETS NECESSITY

Somewhere in the city of New York there are four or five still-unknown objects that belong together. Once together they'll make a work of art. That's Cornell's premise, his metaphysics, and his religion, which I wish to understand.

He sets out from his home on Utopia Parkway without knowing what he is looking for or what he will find. Today it could be something as ordinary and interesting as an old thimble. Years may pass before it has company. In the meantime, Cornell walks and looks. The city has an infinite number of interesting objects in an infinite number of unlikely places.

TERRA INCOGNITA

America still waits to be discovered. Its tramps and poets resemble early navigators setting out on journeys of exploration. Even in its cities there are still places left blank by the map makers.

This afternoon it's a movie house, which, for some reason, is showing two black-and-white horror films. In them the night is always falling. Someone is all alone someplace they shouldn't be. If there's a house, it must be the only one for miles around. If there's a road, it must be deserted. The trees are bare, or if they have leaves, they rustle darkly. The sky still has a little gray light. It is the kind of light in which even one's own hands appear unfamiliar, a stranger's hands.

On the street again, the man in a white suit turning the corner could be the ghost of the dead poet Frank O'Hara.

CLÉO DE MÉRODE

Joseph Cornell could not draw, paint, or sculpt, and yet he was a great American artist.

He roamed the streets of New York from the late 1920s till his death in 1972, foraging in used bookstores and junk shops. "My work was a natural outcome of my love for the city," he said. One day in 1931 he saw some compasses in one shop window and some boxes in the next, and it occurred to him to put them together.

Here are some of the things he found and placed in a box called "L'Égypte de Mlle Cléo de Mérode cours élémentaire d'histoire naturelle," which he constructed in 1940:

Doll's forearm, loose red sand, wood ball, German coin, several glass and mirror fragments, 12 cork-stopped bottles, cutout sphinx head, yellow filaments, 2 intertwined paper spirals, cut-out of Cléo de Mérode's head, cutout of camels and men, loose yellow sand, 6 pearl beads, glass tube with residue of dried green liquid, crumpled tulle, rhinestones, pearl beads, sequins, metal chain, metal and glass fragments, threaded needle, red wood disc, bone and frosted glass fragments, blue celluloid, clear glass crystals, rock specimen, 7 balls, plastic rose petals, three miniature tin spoons for a doll house.

Cléo de Mérode, by the way, was a famous ballerina and femme fatale of the 1890s.

NAKED IN ARCADIA

The New World was already old for Poe. The lost paradise lost again. On a street of faded store signs, Berenice, where was she?

The Church of Divine Metaphysics, with its headquarters in a Bowery storefront, advertises funerals and marriages on a hand-written sign. Around the corner, Salvation Army Store and a junk shop.

America is a place where the Old World shipwrecked. Flea markets and garage sales cover the land. Here's everything the immigrants carried in their suitcases and bundles to these shores and their descendants threw out with the trash:

A pile of Greek 78 records with one Marika Papagika singing; a rubber-doll face of uncertain origin with teeth marks of a child or a small dog; sepia postcards of an unknown city covered with greasy fingerprints; a large empty jewel case lined with black velvet; a menu from a hotel in Palermo serving octopus; an old French book on astronomy with covers and title page missing; a yellowed photograph of a dead Chinese baby.

They should have made them undress and throw their possessions into the sea for the sake of an America where everybody goes naked, it occurs to me. My parents would be naked, too, posing for that picture in the Yellowstone Park with my father's much-prized, Moroccan red fez.

Whitman, too, saw poetry everywhere. In 1912 Apolli-
naire spoke of a new source of inspiration: "Prospec-
tuses, catalogues, posters, advertisements of all sorts"
which contain the poetry of our age.

The history of that idea is familiar and so are its
heroes, Picasso, Arp, Duchamp, Schwitters, Ernst—to
name only a few. You don't make art, you find it. You
accept everything as its material. Schwitters collected
scraps of conversation, newspaper cuttings for his po-
ems. Eliot's *Waste Land* is collage and so are Pound's
Cantos.

The collage technique, that art of reassembling frag-
ments of preexisting images in such a way as to form a
new image, is the most important innovation in the art
of this century. Found objects, chance creations, ready-
mades (mass-produced items promoted into art objects)
abolish the separation between art and life. The com-
monplace is miraculous if rightly seen, if recognized.

"The question is not what you look at, but what you
see," Thoreau writes in his journal. Cornell speaks of
"being plunged into [a] world of complete happiness in
which every triviality becomes imbued with a signifi-
cance..."

Georgio de Chirico, whom Cornell admired im-
mensely, writes: "The huge glove is painted zinc, with
its terrible golden fingernails, swinging over the shop

door in the sad wind blowing on a city afternoon, revealed to me, with its index finger pointing down at the flag stones of the pavement, the hidden signs of the new melancholy."

ARE YOU READY,
MARY BAKER EDDY?

André Breton says in the *Second Surrealist Manifesto:* "Everything tends to make us believe that there exists a certain point of the mind at which life and death, the real and the imagined, past and future, the communicable and the incommunicable, high and low, cease to be perceived as contradictions."

That point is somewhere in the labyrinth, and the labyrinth is the city of New York.

UNTITLED (WINDOW FACADE), CA. 1953–1956

"Is it possible, after all, that in spite of bricks and shaven faces, this world we live in is brimmed with wonders, and I and all mankind, beneath our garbs of common-placeness, conceal enigmas that the stars themselves, and perhaps the highest seraphim, can not resolve?" writes Melville in *Pierre*.

Early Sunday morning in June. It had rained after midnight, and the air and the sky have miraculously cleared. The avenues are empty and the stores closed. A glimpse of things before anyone has seen them.

On the corner an old office building stands vacated. It's being renovated. The walls have been painted and its sixteen windows have been newly washed and now sparkle. Inside there are mirrors and back windows, but no furniture. Everything is very orderly except for a few cracks still visible on the facade and some chipped paint on the sidewalk.

The clarity of one's vision is a work of art.

OUR ANGELIC ANCESTOR

Rimbaud should have gone to America instead of Lake Chad. He'd be a hundred years old and rummaging through a discount store. Didn't he say he liked stupid paintings, signs, popular engravings, erotic books with bad spelling, novels of our grandmothers?

Arthur, poor boy, you would have walked the length of Fourteenth Street and written many more "Illuminations."

Poetry: three mismatched shoes at the entrance of a dark alley.

DIVINE KALEIDOSCOPE

The quest for the lost and the beautiful. Cornell-Orpheus in the city of the soul, the invisible city which occupies the same space as New York.

De Nerval said: "Man has little by little destroyed and cut the eternal type of beauty into a thousand little pieces." Cornell found them in the city and reassembled them. What being is for philosophers, beauty is for Cornell. He writes:

All day long, week in-week out, I look across from my studio table at the forbidding drab gray facade of the huge Manhattan Storage and Warehouse building with its symetrical row after row of double metal blinds, every night, promptly at five, uniformed guards appear simultaneously at each of the myriad windows drawing in the ponderous rivet-studded shutters for the night. But this summer evening at the appointed time the ethereal form of Fanny Cerrito, breathlessly resplendent in gossamer of ondine, appears in each casement to perform the chores of the guards. So guilessly, with such ineffable humility and grace, is the duty discharged as to bring a catch to the throat. Her composure and tender (slow fade-out) glance rebuke regret as she fades from view.

This is extraordinary.

CONEY ISLAND INSIDE EVERY HEAD

Modernism in art and literature gave unparalleled freedom to the individual to invent his or her own world from the parts of the existing one. It abolished the hierarchies of beauty and allowed an assemblage of styles and openness to daily experience. Only such all-inclusive aesthetic could make sense of American reality. Cornell lived these ideas in his art. He experimented with them in the true sense of the word. When Emerson and Thoreau went into the woods, they knew what they were going to find. Cornell preserved the spirit of adventure. He explored the unknown as much as it is possible for any artist and poet to do so.

I WENT TO THE GYPSY

What Cornell sought in his walks in the city, the fortune-tellers already practiced in their parlors. Faces bent over cards, coffee dregs, crystals; divination by contemplation of surfaces which stimulate inner visions and poetic faculties.

De Chirico says: "One can deduce and conclude that every object has two aspects: one current one, which we see nearly always and which is seen by men in general; and the other, which is spectral and metaphysical and seen only by rare individuals in moments of clair-voyance..."

He's right. Here comes the bruja, dressed in black, her lips and fingernails painted blood-red. She saw into the murderer's lovesick heart, and now it's your turn, mister.

OLD POSTCARD OF 42ND STREET
AT NIGHT

I'm looking for the mechanical chess player with a red turban. I hear Pythagoras is there queuing up, and Monsieur Pascal, who hears the silence inside God's ear.

Eternity and time are the coins it requires, everybody's portion of it, for a quick glimpse of that everything which is nothing.

Night of the homeless, the sleepless, night of those winding the watches of their souls, the stopped watches, before the machine with mirrors.

Here's a raised hand covered with dime-store jewels, a hand like "a five-headed Cerberus," and two eyes opened wide in astonishment.

MEDICI SLOT MACHINE

The name enchants, and so does the idea—the juxta-position of the Renaissance boy, the penny arcade, and the Photomat in the subway; what seem at first totally incompatible worlds—but then, of course, we are in Cornell's "magic regions" of Forty-second Street and Times Square.

The boy has the face of one lost in reverie who is about to press his forehead against a windowpane. He has no friends. In the subway there are panhandlers, small-time hustlers, drunks, sailors on leave, teen-aged whores loitering about. The air smells of frying oil, popcorn, and urine. The boy-prince studies the Latin classics and prepares himself for the affairs of the state. He is stubborn and cruel. He already has secret vices. At night he cries himself to sleep. Outside the street is lined with movie palaces showing *films noirs.* One is called *Dark Mirror*, another *Asphalt Jungle.* In them, too, the faces are often in shadow.

"He is as beautiful as a girl," someone says. His pic-ture is repeated in passport size on the machine. Out-side the penny arcade blacks shine shoes, a blind man sells newspapers, young boys in tight jeans hold hands. Everywhere there are vending machines and they all have mirrors. The mad woman goes around scribbling on them with her lipstick. The vending machine is a tattooed bride.

The boy dreams with his eyes open. An angelic image in the dark of the subway. The machine, like any myth, has heterogeneous parts. There must be gear wheels, cogs, and other clever contrivances attached to the crank. Whatever it is, it must be ingenious. Our loving gaze can turn it on. A poetry slot machine offering a jackpot of incommensurable meanings activated by our imagination. Its mystic repertoire has many images. The prince vanishes and other noble children take his place. Lauren Bacall appears for a moment. At 3 A.M. the gum machine on the deserted platform with its freshly wiped mirror is the new wonder-working icon of the Holy Virgin.

A FORCE ILLEGIBLE

Did Cornell know what he was doing? Yes, but mostly no. Does anyone fully? He knew what he liked to see and touch. What he liked, no one was interested in. Surrealism provided him with a way of being more than just an eccentric collector of sundry oddities. The ideas of art came later, if they ever did come clearly. And how could they? His is a practice of divination. Dada and surrealism gave him a precedent and a freedom. I have in mind especially their astonishing discovery that lyric poetry can come out of chance operations. Cornell believed in the same magic, and he was right! All art is a magic operation, or, if you prefer, a prayer for a new image.

"In murky corners of old cities where everything—horror, too—is magical," Baudelaire writes. The city is a huge image machine. A slot machine for the solitaries. Coins of reverie, of poetry, secret passion, religious madness, it converts them all. A force illegible.

II

The Little Box

THE OLD MAN TOLD ME

There was a movie theater here once. It played silent films. It was like watching the world through dark glasses on a rainy evening.

One night the piano player mysteriously disappeared. We were left with the storming sea that made no sound, and a beautiful woman on a long, empty beach whose tears rolled down silently as she watched me falling asleep in my mother's arms.

They talked of "Beauty" and "Truth" in those far-off days. No one sneezed in the music room. Loving couples were made of Italian marble. Our "goddess" had huge white wings made of lightest gauze. She played the piano, favoring the black keys. Her lover's hands fluttered; his sighs flew heavenward. Everywhere one met with upraised eyes. The old women hid behind their fans where they turned into tall vases.

O sunsets and golden domes! The liveried servants tiptoed in and out, their mouths sewn shut with red thread. In their hands they carried death masks of famous poets. There was one for everyone to wear while the tea was being poured.

All of a sudden they all vanished. The clock in which Time sits like a prisoner shifted its chains. There was only a love seat left with its paws of a wild animal and a smell of smoke at twilight. Old chimney fires put out by long autumn rains.

MATCHBOX WITH A FLY IN IT

Shadow box
Music box
Pill box
A box which contains a puzzle
A box with tiny drawers,
Navigation box
Jewelry box
Sailor's box
Butterfly box
Box stuffed with souvenirs of a sea voyage
Magic prison
An empty box

"SOLITUDE, MY MOTHER, TELL ME MY LIFE AGAIN"

—O. V. DE L. MILOSZ

Abandoned children's games in the little side street, the Street of Lost Steps, with the chalk lines of hopscotch in the late afternoon sunlight and shadow.

In antiquity the game symbolized the labyrinth in which one kicked a small flat white stone—one's soul —toward the exit, the vanishing point with its cloudless sky.

DOG WEARING BABY CLOTHES

Here's how Cornell described the contents of some 150 files he kept at home:

a diary journal repository laboratory, picture gallery, museum, sanctuary, observatory, key... the core of a labyrinth, a clearinghouse for dreams and visions... childhood regained.

Someone else, not knowing Cornell's method and purpose, would describe what's inside the files as the contents of a trash basket, agreeing, perhaps, that this is the strangest trash imaginable, for there are things in it that could have been discarded by a nineteenth-century Parisian as well as the twentieth-century American.

BIRDS OF A FEATHER

Cornell loved Houdini, who was famous for escaping from ingeniously constructed boxes. The boxes had secret trapdoors and exits and could be dropped in the sea with Houdini variously bound and chained in them. Some said Houdini made his escapes by dematerializing himself and then resuming his human form.

That art is called illusionist. Illusionists make it *seem*. It appears that the lady in the coffin is being sawn in half, except she isn't. There are two points to make about this: (1) philosophically, illusionism is a theory that the material world is an illusion; (2) illusionism is a technique of using images to deceive. It raises the question of whether perception can give us true and direct knowledge of the world. Psychologists, for instance, have constructed a "distorted room" in which a grown man appears to be the size of an infant. Other examples are funhouse mirrors and the conjurer's sleight of hand. Cinema, of course, is the most successful illusionist's trick yet.

The eyes cannot be philosophically trusted, but in the meantime they can be entertained. Nature, too, makes fakes—fake masterpieces of art, we should say. All these splendid sunsets are mere illusions and cannot be true of real objects and properties. The evening sky and the big city in the distance are constantly changing their theatrical scenery. We don't really believe any of this, but it sure looks that way sometimes.

POSTAGE STAMP WITH A PYRAMID

The lonely boy must play quietly because his parents are sleeping after lunch. He kneels on the floor between their beds pushing a matchbox, inside which he imagines himself sitting. The day is hot. In her sleep his mother has uncovered her breasts like the Sphinx. The car, for that's what it is, is moving very slowly because its wheels are sinking in the deep sand. Ahead, nothing but wind, sky, and more sand.

"Shush," says the father sternly to the desert wind.

THE LITTLE BOX

The little box gets her first teeth
And her little length
Little width little emptiness
And all the rest she has

The little box continues growing
The cupboard that she was inside
Is now inside her

And she grows bigger bigger bigger
Now the room is inside her
And the house and the city and the earth
And the world she was in before

The little box remembers her childhood
And by a great great longing
She becomes a little box again

Now in the little box
You have the whole world in miniature
You can easily put it in a pocket
You can easily steal it easily lose it

Take care of the little box.

—Vasko Popa

Perhaps the ideal way to observe the boxes is to place them on the floor and lie down beside them.

It is not surprising that child faces stare out of the boxes and that they have the dreamy look of children at play. Theirs is the happy solitude of a time without clocks when children are masters of their world. Cornell's boxes are reliquaries of days when imagination reigned. They are inviting us, of course, to start our childhood reveries all over again.

VAUDEVILLE DE LUXE

My baby's got a black cat bone.

—Hop Wilson

A fetish, so the dictionaries tell us, is a spirit attached to a material object. "Hide your God, He's your strength," advised the poet Paul Valéry, and the same goes for the fetish. It's usually kept out of sight.

Cornell's boxes are like witch doctors' concoctions. They contain objects that have sacred and magical properties. The box is a little voodoo temple with an altar. Love medicine or medicine of immortality is being prepared.

In the meantime, you've got to whisper to the black cat bone if you want to make it do its thing.

UNTITLED (WHITE BALLS IN COTS), CA. MID-1950

This box has the appearance of a game board, a puzzle, or perhaps some abacuslike calculating machine. The balls have stopped randomly on their own, or they were moved by an invisible hand. Whichever is the case, this is their position now. In other boxes of the same series, balls may be replaced by blocks and their position varies.

It's been a long time since the balls were in motion, one thinks. Besides, some of them appear to be missing. Here's an image of infinity, not as extension, but as division into equal and anonymous parts.

How's this terrifying game to be played?

Around the boxes I can still hear Cornell mumble to himself. In the basement of the quiet house on Utopia Parkway he's passing the hours by changing the positions of a few items, setting them in new positions relative to one another in a box. At times the move is no more than a tenth of an inch. At other times, he picks the object, as one would a chess figure, and remains long motionless, lost in complicated deliberation.

Many of the boxes make me think of those chess problems in which no more than six to seven figures are left on the board. The caption says: "White mates in two moves," but the solution escapes the closest scrutiny. As anyone who attempts to solve these problems knows, the first move is the key, and it's bound to be an unlikely appearing move.

I have often cut a chess problem from a newspaper and taped it to the wall by my bed so that I may think about it first thing in the morning and before turning off the lights at night. I have especially been attracted to problems with minimum numbers of figures, the ones that resemble the ending of some long, complicated, and evenly fought game. It's the subtlety of two minds scheming that one aims to recover.

At times, it may take months to reach the solution, and in a few instances I was never able to solve the problem. The board and its figures remained as mysterious as ever. Unless there was an error in instructions or position, or a misprint, there was no way in hell the white could mate in two moves. And yet...

At some point my need for a solution was replaced by the poetry of my continuous failure. The white queen remained where it was on the black square, and so did the other figures in the original places, eternally, whenever I closed my eyes.

A toy is a trap for dreamers. The true toy is a poetic object.

There's an early sculpture of Giacometti's called The Palace at 4 A.M. (1932). It consists of no more than a few sticks assembled into a spare scaffolding, which the mysterious title makes haunting and unforgettable. Giacometti said that it was a dream house for him and the woman with whom he was in love.

These are dreams that a child would know. Dreams in which objects are renamed and invested with imaginary lives. A pebble becomes a human being. Two sticks leaning against each other make a house. In that world one plays the game of being someone else.

This is what Cornell is after, too. How to construct a vehicle of reverie, an object that would enrich the imagination of the viewer and keep him company forever.

UNTITLED (BÉBÉ MARIE), EARLY 1940S

The chubby doll in a forest of twigs. Her eyes are open and her lips and cheeks are red. While her mother was busy with other things, she went to her purse, took out the makeup, and painted her face in front of a mirror. Now she's to be punished.

A spoiled little girl wearing a straw hat about to be burnt at the stake. One can already see the flames in her long hair entangled with the twigs. Her eyes are wide open so she can watch us watching her.

All this is vaguely erotic and sinister.

SECRET TOY

You make unknown the child's sleeping face, his half-open eyes and mouth.

Everything in his world is a secret, and the games are still the game of love, the game of hide-and-seek, and the chilly game of solitude.

In a secret room in a secret house his secret toy sits listening to its own stillness.

Crows fly over that city. The ghosts of his and our dreams come together at night like window dressers and their mannequins on a street of dark, abandoned buildings and white clouds.

2

3

4

CARTE GÉOGRAPHIQUE DE LA LUNE

8

THE MAGIC STUDY OF HAPPINESS

In the smallest theater in the world the bread crumbs speak. It's a mystery play on the subject of a lost paradise. Once there was a kitchen with a table on which a few crumbs were left. Through the window you could see your young mother by the fence talking to a neighbor. She was cold and kept hugging her thin dress tighter and tighter. The clouds in the sky sailed on as she threw her head back to laugh.

Where the words can't go any further—there's the hard table. The crumbs are watching you as you in turn watch them. The unknown in you and the unknown in them attract each other. The two unknowns are like illicit lovers when they're exceedingly and unaccountably happy.

CIGARS CLAMPED BETWEEN
THEIR TEETH

I've read that Goethe, Hans Christian Andersen, and Lewis Carroll were managers of their own miniature theaters. There must have been many other such playhouses in the world. We study the history and literature of the period, but we know nothing about these plays that were being performed for an audience of one.

O FADING MEMORY!

It seems we learn something about art when we experience what the word solitude *is meant to designate.*
— Maurice Blanchot

In my childhood, toy shops still sold miniature theaters made of cardboard. The scenery, the actors, the musicians, and the rest of the props came printed on colored sheets of paper sold separately. One would cut the figures out, mount them on cardboard, and then move them around the stage by means of grooves in the floor. There was even a red curtain that opened or closed. I never owned one of these theaters, but I saw them assembled at other people's homes.

I had two very strange old maiden aunts in Belgrade whom my mother and I used to visit from time to time. They lived in a small cluttered house. There was so much furniture—the inheritance of generations of dead relatives—that each room was a maze. One had to squeeze between huge wardrobes, be told repeatedly to be careful of the many knickknacks collecting dust on shelves and tables of all sizes and shapes. Once, having lost my way in that maze, I came upon a paper theater all set up. I don't remember if I was told whose it was. Usually boys played with them and the girls had dollhouses, so I immediately assumed this was a theater of some dead boy. Beautiful Marina, the younger of the two aunts, showed me how to move the figures. Marina was insane. I know that now and suspected it even then. In any case, she'd put her finger on her lips to tell me to be quiet. The house was already so quiet one could hear a pin drop while I moved the figures and she watched intently. I remember the dolls' bright-colored costumes and fixed stares. That day's backdrop was a dark forest, the kind you read about in fairy tales. Above there was a moon half hidden by the clouds. The paper actors were all smiling in an identical way. My mother told me on the way home that my aunts had boxes full of old dolls. I knew they were all smiling, too.

My own theater did not come from a store. It consisted of a few broken toy soldiers made of clay and an assortment of small wooden blocks, corks, and other unidentifiable objects which, in my imagination, had acquired anthropomorphic properties. My stage was under the table. My figures enacted what could only be described as an endless saga of the Wild West. There was a hero, his best friend, the bad guy, the Indians, but I don't remember the heroine. I was seven or eight years old. The war was just over. There was little to do but imagine.

THE MEMORY THEATER
OF GIULIO CAMILLO

"The work is of wood [continued Viglius], marked with many images and full of little boxes."

"He [Camillo] pretends that all things that the human mind can conceive and which we cannot see with the corporeal eye, after being collected together by diligent meditation, may be expressed by certain corporeal signs in such a way that the beholder may at once perceive with his eyes everything that is otherwise hidden in the depths of the human mind. And it is because of this corporeal looking that he calls it theater."

"[T]he final secret of [Camillo's] work is magical, mystical, belonging to the occult philosophy, impossible to explain to a rational enquirer, like his friend Erasmus, under whose eye the Idea of the Memory Theater dissolves into stammering incoherence."

UNTITLED (PINK PALACE), CA. 1946–1948

Another oneiric playhouse. A phantom palace in a for-est of bare trees, hoar frost and night. A fabulous palace disproportionately large to the size of the figures stand-ing in front of it. They are tiny and indistinct and would require many enlargements before one could see the expression of their faces. Many appear to be soldiers and they seem agitated. They point to one another. Some sort of news has arrived. One of them is probably the messenger.

One is reminded of eighteenth-century engravings of city scenes, towers of London or the palaces of Venice rising serenely above the microscopic figures one imag-ines were strolling the day the artist drew the scene.

THE MOON IS THE SORCERER'S
HELPER

As the curtain goes up we see a forest with tall, fantastic trees. It is night. There's a moon half hidden by the clouds. Blue mist drifts through the trees. The forest is a place in which everything your heart desires and fears lives.

"Blue is the color of your yellow hair," said Schwitters. He walked into a forest near Hanover and found there half of a toy train engine, which he then used in one of his collages.

Beauty is about the improbable coming true suddenly. The great ballerina, Emma Livry, a protégée of Taglioni, for instance, died in flames while dancing the role of a night butterfly.

UNTITLED (SOAP BUBBLE SET), 1936

A soap bubble went to meet infinity.

Here's a cabinet containing the implements you need. There's a classroom map of the moon, a clay pipe, a blue egg in a wineglass, and a child's head on a block of wood. There are many versions of this dream machine, but the map, the pipe, and the glass are almost always present.

The heavenly bodies are soap bubbles. They float in the empyrean, cradling the dreamer. The ephemeral bubble ascends into the wintry cold and silence of the sky. It's the soul of the world ascending. Cosmogenies are soap bubbles. The father of our solitude is a child. A soap bubble has no content. After it has burst, there's nothing left of it.

The leap of a ballet dancer is a soap bubble, too. "Our hearts leap," we say. This is the "long bright silence" of Nietzsche's before which we stand in awe. The far and beyond and the near momentarily touch. The world is beautiful but not sayable. That's why we need art.

THESE ARE POETS WHO SERVICE
CHURCH CLOCKS

Many people have already speculated about the relation-
ship between play and the sacred. The light of reverie,
let us note, is a dim light. The near darkness of old
churches and old movies is that of dreams. Our mem-
ories are divine images because memory is not subject
to the ordinary laws of time and space. Making deities
is what we do in our reverie. Images surrounded by
shadow and silence. Silence is that vast, cosmic church
in which we always stand alone. Silence is the only
language God speaks.

III
Imaginary Hotels

WHAT MOZART SAW ON MULBERRY STREET

If you love watching movies from the middle on, Cornell is your director. It's those first moments of some already-started, unknown movie with its totally mysterious images and snatches of dialogue before the setting and even the vaguest hint of a plot became apparent that he captures.

Cornell spliced images and sections from preexisting Hollywood films he found in junk stores. He made cinema collages guided only by the poetry of images. Everything in them has to do with ellipses. Actors speak but we don't know to whom. Scenes are interrupted. What one remembers are images.

He also made a movie from the point of view of a bust of Mozart in a store window. Here, too, chance is employed. People pass on the street and some of them stop to look in the window. Marcel Duchamp and John Cage use chance operation to get rid of the subjectivity of the artist. For Cornell it's the opposite. To submit to chance is to reveal the self and its obsessions. In that sense Cornell is not a dadaist or a surrealist. He believes in charms and good luck.

THE GAZE WE KNEW AS A CHILD

"People who look for symbolic meaning fail to grasp the inherent poetry and mystery of the images," writes René Magritte, and I could not agree more. Nevertheless, this requires some clarification. There are really three kinds of images. first, there are those seen with eyes open in the manner of realists in both art and literature. Then there are images we see with eyes closed. Romantic poets, surrealists, expressionists, and everyday dreamers know them. The images Cornell has in his boxes are, however, of the third kind. They partake of both dream and reality, and of something else that doesn't have a name. They tempt the viewer in two opposite directions. One is to look and admire the elegance and other visual properties of the composition, and the other is to make up stories about what one sees. In Cornell's art, the eye and the tongue are at cross purposes. Neither one by itself is sufficient. It's that mingling of the two that makes up the third image.

UTOPIA CUISINE

It's raining on Utopia Parkway. The invalid brother is playing with his toy trains. Cornell is reading the sermons of John Donne, and the box of the Hôtel Beau-Séjour is baking in the oven like one of his mother's pies.

In order to make them appear aged, Cornell would give his boxes eighteen to twenty coats of paint, varnish them, polish them, and leave them in the sun and rain. He also baked them to make them crack and look old.

Forgers of antiquities, lovers of times past, employ the same method.

TOTEMISM

Inside everyone there are secret rooms. They're cluttered and the lights are out. There's a bed in which someone is lying with his face to the wall. In his head there are more rooms. In one, the venetian blinds shake in the approaching summer storm. Every once in a while an object on the table becomes visible: a broken compass, a pebble the color of midnight, an enlargement of a school photograph with a face in the back circled, a watch spring—each one of these items is a totem of the self.

Every art is about the longing of One for the Other. Orphans that we are, we make our sibling kin out of anything we can find. The labor of art is the slow and painful metamorphosis of the One into the Other.

CORNELL'S WHITE NIGHTS

"A room that is like a reverie."

—Baudelaire

Insomnia is an all-night travel agency with posters advertising faraway places. There the sea is always blue and so is the sky. A little white hotel with green shutters waits for you, each one of its rooms "a thing of twilight, bluish and roseate."

Like a traveler weary of his journeying, you undress with the window open. The setting sun wears a red turban. The sea is dark blue. In the lush garden swallows are darting. When the night finally falls, veiled Scheherazade will bring mint tea to your bed.

In the meantime, silence and your shadow on the bare wall.

IMAGINARY HOTELS

There is the Hôtel Beau-Séjour, Hôtel des Etrangers, Grand Hôtel de la Pomme d'Or, Hôtel du Nord, and many more. The man who never traveled made up his own Baedecker.

Cornell's hotels are somewhere in southern France or in the French colonies in North Africa. They've all seen better days. Once they had white columns, motionless servants, marble statues from which now only pedestals remain.

You're invited to imagine your own: an old hotel in New Orleans with paint peeling and laundry hanging on its white porches; or a pink motel in the Nevada desert with a single pickup truck parked outside one of its rooms, and no one in sight for miles around.

POSTCARDS FROM FARAWAY PLACES

1

We visited a museum in Labrador. The walls of every room were blank except for the shadows we cast as the sun went down over the frozen landscape.

2

The undertakers in S. sell toys in their funeral parlors. There are beach balls and stuffed animals in open coffins and electric trains going in circles on the floor drawing many children and grownups to their doors.

3

In the desert, we heard of birds that walk on stilts and built circus tents instead of nests.

4

As darkness fell, our host, the Prince, went to stand on the parapet of his palazzo with his beard on fire.

5

The other day in Z., we met the blind painter of doll faces and ate dragon stew.

CENTURIES OF JUNE

A safe haven, a nook, a place out of sight in which to snuggle. Every dreamer crawls into his corner. Like an escapee, he thinks only of hiding and disappearing. In every cranny in the world someone has burrowed to seek solace. From the crack in the wall he glimpses the world from which he is absent.

The pursuers enter the hotel room and there's no one there. The one they're looking for hasn't been born yet, or he has been dead for a hundred years. The sunlight falling through the open window knows that. Soon they're gone and the room is again empty like the morning sky. Within that single instant, "Centuries of June," as Emily Dickinson said.

SLEEPWALKER'S TRAVEL GUIDE

The Grand Hotel of The Universe with its tower clock stopped.

The shrouded chairs and sofas in the Hotel of Bad Dreams.

The cry of love in the Hotel of the Eternal Moment.

Hotel of the Bloody Revolution on the Avenue of Fates and Furies. Two black shoes with worn heels left under its entrance awning.

Our dead grandmother staring at an empty plate in the Hotel of the Great Secret.

On the same street, Hotel of the Erased Name. St. Sebastian pierced by arrows at the open door. St. Lucie holding her eyes on a plate in one of the high, sun-bloodied windows.

And on the corner, the angel of death in a yellow taxi rounding up guests for the Hotel Night Sky.

RUE PARADIS

A hotel frequented by phantoms. One never sees any-
one arrive, anyone leave. The dim lobby with potted
palms is deserted. The desk clerk is gone and so are all
the keys. Still, everything appears in immaculate order.
The thick rugs on the floor, the sofas and little tables,
the monumental mirrors on the walls. The rooms, it's
whispered, have mirrors even on the ceiling. The great
Marie Taglioni is somewhere up there among miles
and miles of intersecting silent corridors, and so is the
acrobat Blondin, Dr. Caligari, Miss Dickinson, young
Louise Brooks, and so many other dead dancers, ac-
tresses, and poets. In the bridal suite there's no one, but
its windows are open. In the afternoon quiet, one can
hear from across the street the tapping of a solitary
crutch in the children's hospital.

THE IMPERSONAL SUBJECT
OF THE VERB "TO BE"

Since the "it" in our existence cannot be further identified, since the essence of language is its poverty in the face of "it," since one cannot hold a mirror to "it," since "it" is the monster in the labyrinth and the eternal playmate, one strives for an art whose aim is to render the effect of "its" presence.

STREET-CORNER THEOLOGY

It ought to be clear that Cornell is a religious artist. Vision is his subject. He makes holy icons. He proves that one needs to believe in angels and demons even in a modern world in order to make sense of it.

The disorder of the city is sacred. All things are interrelated. As above, so below. We are fragments of an unutterable whole. Meaning is always in search of itself. Unsuspected revelations await us around the next corner.

The blind preacher and his old dog are crossing the street against the oncoming traffic of honking cabs and trucks. He carries his guitar in a beat-up case taped with white tape so it looks like it's bandaged.

Making art in America is about saving one's soul.

HOTEL AT THE END OF THE WORLD

"You have no secrets from your insomnia," says the sign at the entrance. The wall in your room is white and so are the sheets and pillows. There's a casement, a grating high up on the ceiling, as if once the hotel was a prison.

White truth, "immensity cloistered," as Donne said.

Infinity: Time that has no story to tell.

You have the feeling that you are measuring the All with your own small piece of string. Perhaps the torn end of a shoelace?

That is why Cornell's final boxes are nearly empty.

PART OF THE MISSING WHOLE

Empty space and silence. The city like a chessboard on which the few remaining figures are motionless and un-named. Inside the white buildings, more empty space and silence.

Vacant rooms, blank walls, effaced signs, deserted hallways, X-ed doors, untenanted cells, birdless aviaries.

Poetry of absence, poetry of the minimum, pieces of the lost world.

APOLLINARIS. Apollo, god of light. Apollinaire the poet, who loved street performers, musicians with cornets and tambourines, tightrope walkers, jugglers.

Here's the long pole given to us by the god of sleep-walkers. Here's the hoop of the dead girl and the parrot and the cockatoo that flew out of the pet shop into the snow when we were little.

Emptiness, this divine condition, this school of metaphysics.

> A small white ball
> In a bare, whitewashed room
> With a QUIET sign.

EMILY DICKINSON

Cornell and Dickinson are both in the end unknowable. They live within the riddle, as Dickinson would say. Their biographies explain nothing. They are without precedent, eccentric, original, and thoroughly American. If her poems are like his boxes, a place where secrets are kept, his boxes are like her poems, the place of unlikely things coming together.

They both worry about their souls' salvation. Voyagers and explorers of their own solitudes, they make them vast, make them cosmic. They are religious artists in a world in which old metaphysics and aesthetic ideas were eclipsed. To read her poems, to look at his boxes, is to begin to think in a new way about American literature and art.

DESERTED PERCH, 1949

The bird has flown. There's only the perch left, a dropped feather, a watch spring, and a crack, "the very tiny crack in which another world begins and ends," as Slavko Mihalić says.

Illusionist art, sleight of hand.

"[E]terniday," as Cornell would say.

Wednesday, September 21, 1949

> *working all morning—taking a rest in the chair in the back yard—all of a sudden an overwhelming sense of harmony and complete happiness, a spontaneous lifting that seemed like a healing dispensing with specific work for the time being in this blissful state.*

Notes

All quotations from Cornell's journals come from the collection of his papers on microfilm in the Archives of American Art–Smithsonian Institution.

Page 3 Gérard de Nerval, *Selected Writings*, translated by Geoffrey Wagner. Ann Arbor: University of Michigan Press, 1970.

Page 8 Papers of Joseph Cornell, Archives of American Art–Smithsonian Institution.

Page 10 Edgar Allan Poe, *Poetry and Tales*. New York: The Library of America, 1984.

Page 13 Papers of Joseph Cornell, Archives of American Art–Smithsonian Institution.

Page 16 Papers of Joseph Cornell, Archives of American Art–Smithsonian Institution. Cléo de Mérode was a ballerina of La Belle Epoque and a mistress of King Leopold II.

Page 19 Guillaume Apollinaire, *Apollinaire on Art, Essays and Reviews 1902–1918*, edited by Le Roy C. Brevnig. New York: The Viking Press, 1972. Henry David Thoreau, *Selected Journals of Henry David Thoreau*. New York: Signet, 1967. Papers of Joseph Cornell, Archives of American Art–Smithsonian Institution. Giorgio de Chirico from *Theories of Modern Art*, edited by Hershel B. Chip. Berkeley: University of California Press, 1968.

Page 21 André Breton, *Manifestoes of Surrealism*. Ann Arbor: University of Michigan Press, 1974.

Page 22 Herman Melville. *Pierre, or the Ambiguities, and Other Works*. New York: Library of America, 1984.

Page 24 Gérard de Nerval, *Selected Writings*. Papers of Joseph Cornell, Archives of American Art–Smithsonian Institution. Fanny Cerrito was a legendary nineteenth-century ballerina, and Cornell's favorite. Her contemporary, the French poet Théophile Gautier, said of her: "Undines, Sylphides, and Salamanders will not cavil at her rendering of them."

Page 26 Giorgio de Chirico is quoted from *Metaphysical Art* by Massimo Carra. New York: Praeger, 1971.

Page 30 Charles Baudelaire, *The flowers of Evil,* translated by Richard Howard. Boston: David R. Godine, 1982.

Page 36 I found this line from Oscar Venceslas de Lubicz Milosz in an old notebook of mine.

Page 39 Papers of Joseph Cornell, Archives of American Art–Smithsonian Institution.

Page 40 Vasko Popa, *Homage to the Lame Wolf,* translated by Charles Simic. Oberlin: Oberlin College Press, 1971.

Page 42 Hop Wilson, from a blues song. Paul Valéry, *The Art of Poetry.* Princeton: Princeton University Press, 1958.

Page 51 Maurice Blanchot, *The Space of Literature.* Lincoln: University of Nebraska Press, 1989.

Page 53 Francis Yates, *The Art of Memory.* Chicago: University of Chicago Press, 1966.

Page 55 John Elderfield, *Kurt Schwitters.* New York: Thames and Hudson, 1985.

Page 62 René Magritte is quoted from *Twentieth-Century Artists on Art*, edited by Dore Ashton. New York: Pantheon, 1985.

Page 65 Charles Baudelaire, *Twenty Prose Poems*, translated by Michael Hamburger. San Francisco: City Lights Books, 1988.

Page 68 Emily Dickinson, *The Complete Poems*, edited by Thomas H. Johnson. Boston: Little, Brown and Co., 1960.

Page 70 Marie Taglioni, another legendary nineteenth-century ballerina. Blondin was a famous acrobat. Dr. Caligari is the hero of the silent German film classic *The Cabinet of Dr. Caligari*. Louise Brooks was a silent-movie actress.

Page 76 Slavko Mihalić, Croatian poet, translated by Charles Simic. Papers of Joseph Cornell, Archives of American Art–Smithsonian Institution.

ABOUT THE AUTHOR

Charles Simic is a poet, essayist and translator. He has published twenty collections of his own poetry, five books of essays, a memoir, and numerous of books of translations. He has received many literary awards for his poems and his translations, including the Pulitzer Prize, the Griffin Prize and the MacArthur Fellowship. *Voice at 3 A.M.*, his selected later and new poems, was published in 2003 and a new book of poems *My Noiseless Entourage* came out in the spring of 2005.

Titles in Series